Hidden Treasure

by Geoffrey Trease

illustrated by Chris Molan
and with photographs

Lodestar Books   E. P. Dutton   New York

Originally published in Great Britain 1989 by
Hamish Hamilton Children's Books

First published in the United States 1989 by
E. P. Dutton, New York, New York,
a division of NAL Penguin Inc.

Designer: Gillian Riley
Editor: Felicity Trotman
Printed in Hong Kong by Imago Publishing
First Edition COBE 10 9 8 7 6 5 4 3 2 1

Conceived, designed and produced by
Belitha Press Ltd
31 Newington Green, London N16 9PU

The publishers wish to thank the following for permission to
reproduce copyright material:

Robert Harding Picture Library, title page (leopard), pp 6, 8 *centre*,
14 *all*, 15 *left*, 21 *top*, 22 *both*, 24, 25 *bottom right*, 26, 27, 40, 42 *top
left*, 43.
Picturepoint, pp 12, 21 *bottom right*, 25 *bottom left*.
BBC Hulton Picture Library, pp 6, 11 *bottom left*, 25 *top right*.
The Mansell Collection, pp 7 *all*, 8 *left*, 10, 11 *right*, 20 *both*.
The British Museum, pp 16, 17, 28, 29, 30, 34, 35.
National Museum, Athens, title page (gold mask), pp 13, 15 *right*.
Ministry of Tourism and Information, Ankara, p 9.
Peabody Museum, Harvard University, title page (monkey), pp. 37,
38, 39, photographed by Hillel Burger.
Society for Anglo-Chinese Understanding, p 42 *bottom right*.
South American Pictures, pp 44, 46.

Maps and diagrams by Gillian Riley

Library of Congress Cataloging-in-Publication Data

Trease, Geoffrey, date
    Hidden treasure / by Geoffrey Trease;
    illustrated by Chris Molan.
        p.   cm.—(Time detectives)
    Includes index.
    Summary: Discusses great archeological digs in
    such places as Troy, Sutton Hoo, and the tomb of
    Tutankhamen, and describes some of the
    treasures thus discovered.
    ISBN 0-525-67270-2
    1. Antiquities—Juvenile literature.
    2. Archeology—History—Juvenile literature.
    3. Civilization, Ancient—Juvenile literature.
    4. Treasure-trove—History—Juvenile literature.
    [1. Antiquities.   2. Archeology—History.
    3. Buried Treasure—History.]
    I. Molan, Chris, ill.   II. Title.   III. Series.
CC171.T74   1989   88-21699
930—dc19   CIP
                                                   AC

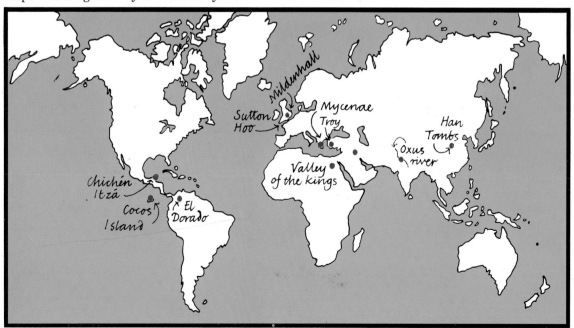

Contents

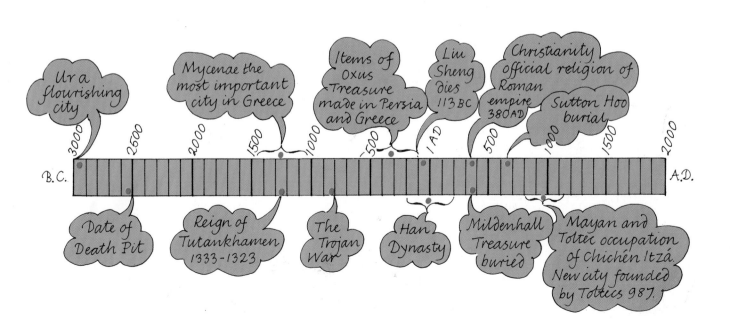

Introduction   The Hunt for Gold

All London was in panic that June of 1667.

Dutch warships had sailed into the mouth of the Thames and sunk the British fleet. It looked as if the city itself might be captured by the enemy.

Samuel Pepys (say *"peeps"*) could not leave his post at the navy office. But he sent all his money, in bags of gold, down to his old father's house at Brampton in Huntingdonshire. One Sunday morning, his wife and his father waited until they thought all the neighbors would be at church. Then they went out into the garden and buried the money in broad daylight.

Poor Pepys nearly went mad when he heard how careless they had been. It was several months before he had a chance to go down to Brampton himself to see if his gold was still safe.

He waited for darkness. He went into the garden with his father—and the old man could not remember just where the money had been buried.

Pepys wrote in his diary how he "began heartily to sweat, and be angry" as he poked around in the soil by the light of a shaded lantern. At last he saw the glint of some gold pieces, but the bags had rotted and split in the damp earth, spilling the coins everywhere.

Pepys toiled until two o'clock in the morning and found forty-five of the coins. The next day, with his clerk's help, he went carefully through all the loose earth with pails and a sieve. He found another thirty-four. He reckoned he had accounted for most of the money.

He was lucky. The Dutch invaders had not attacked London. He had lived to dig up his own treasure again.

Down the ages countless people have hurriedly buried their treasure when there was a war or a revolution. Many of them never came back to dig it up again. There must be a good deal that remains to be found.

There are other explanations for hidden treasure.

There are the hoards of loot concealed by pirates and thieves who never returned to collect it. There is treasure that was accidentally lost and covered over in some catastrophe like a great flood or a volcanic eruption. And there are the fantastic treasures that nobody ever intended to come back for—like the wealth buried in the tomb of an Egyptian king or a Chinese princess, so that the dead person would have it ready for use in some other world.

The stories in this book are all true. Many of the wonderful objects are displayed in famous museums all over the world.

"out again about midnight (for it was now grown so late) and did make shift to gather 45 pieces more."
Pepys' Diary, *October 10, 1667*

1 The Jewels of Helen

Heinrich Schliemann, aged about forty-eight. Scholars laughed at his idea that the story of the Trojan war was true, and that the city could be found.

Part of Troy as it is today. With the remains of nine cities on one site, it is still hard to work out the relationship between the layers. No wonder Schliemann was confused, and dug straight through the city he was really looking for!

The Treasure of Troy

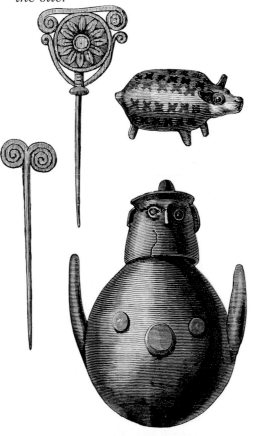

Schliemann's workmen—anything from 80 to 160 a day—excavating the site.

The tale of Troy is one of the oldest in the world. A Trojan prince, Paris, ran away with Helen, the wondrously beautiful wife of the Spartan king, Menelaus. His brother Agamemnon and all the other Greek kings, Achilles and Ajax and Odysseus, joined forces to besiege Troy. After ten years they got inside by a trick. They built a huge horse of wood and left it outside the gates, full of armed men. Then the Greeks pretended to give up the siege and go away. The delighted Trojans dragged the wooden horse into the city, though it was too big to go through the gates and they had to break down the wall. When they were tired with their rejoicings and were all asleep, the Greeks burst out of their hiding place and set the city on fire, while their main army came back in the darkness and rushed through the gap in the walls. Troy was burned to the ground.

The story is told in Homer's poem, the *Iliad*, composed about 800 B.C. but not written down until two centuries later.

History or fiction? Was there ever a real Troy?

A German, Heinrich Schliemann, used to describe how he was fascinated by the story as a small boy, and vowed there and then to find the vanished city when he grew up. But Schliemann was a great spinner of yarns—an enthusiast whose fancies ran away with him. He does not seem to have mentioned this childhood vow to anyone at the time.

FACT BOX

The site of Troy lies in Turkey, near the mouth of the Dardanelles, facing across the Aegean Sea to Greece.

Nine cities were built there between about 3000 B.C. and A.D. 500.

The famous Troy was destroyed about 1200 B.C.

The site was first excavated by Heinrich Schliemann, a rich German businessman, between 1870 and 1890.

The treasure he found disappeared in Germany in 1945.

Yet, many years later, he certainly *was* the man who proved that Troy had indeed existed.

He was forty-six when he first saw the place. He had already made a fortune in business in America, Russia and elsewhere. Some of his dealings had not always been entirely straightforward. A bullet-headed little man with a round face and a mustache, Schliemann had stupendous energy. He had no deep education; he was humbly respectful to people he regarded as real scholars, but he had picked up a dozen foreign languages.

It was not all poetry and legend on "the ringing plains of windy Troy." Ordinary folk once lived there, not only armor-clad heroes, as is shown by the homely articles turned up by Schliemann's workmen. Among them was this perforated disc or "whorl" used in spinning thread—it gave extra momentum to the spindle as it went round and round. Animal figures are cut into it.
Two-handled jars and pots with lids were commonly found. One has small holes pierced in the sides. On the previous page is the so-called Minerva Vase, named after the goddess of wisdom (in Greek, Athena), but hardly flattering if meant to represent her.

Frank Calvert, an Englishman living in Turkey, thought that the Troy of legend lay inside a great mound called Hisarlik, rising 130 feet (40 meters) above the flat plain. Schliemann had his doubts, but he got a permit from the Turkish government and began to dig in 1870.

It was lucky that he was rich. Sometimes he had 160 workmen digging huge trenches across the mound. The excavations were spread over four years, with about nine months of active work altogether. Hundreds of tons of earth were shoveled away—enough to prove that there *had* been a city underneath, but also enough to do terrible damage that could never be put right.

It was not Schliemann's fault. No one in those days understood scientific archeology.

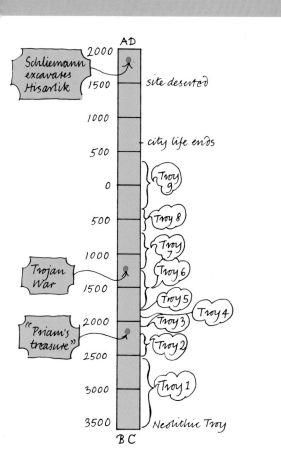

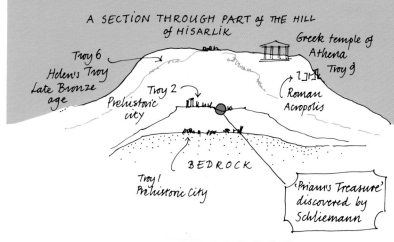

As centuries pass, a ruin gets covered with a stratum of rubbish and new soil. Fresh buildings may be put up. In time their ruins are built upon again. The site becomes a sort of layer cake. Thus, the remains of Roman London have been found deep below modern office buildings. Modern archeologists must note exactly where each object was lying when found. Especially, how deep. The rule is, the deeper the older.

Schliemann knew nothing of this. His peasant laborers dug away, knocking down ancient walls, muddling everything up, and destroying valuable evidence forever. Schliemann proved that there had been four cities built one after another—later he found six and actually there had been nine.

He was wrong in thinking that the Troy of Homer's poem was the second stratum from the bottom. His workmen had dug straight through that Troy, and he was looking at the traces of a city a thousand years older.

Part of an ornate diadem, among thousands of gold items that Schliemann imagined to have been the jewelry of the runaway Spartan queen, Helen.

9

Sophie Schliemann, wearing the jewels of Helen. The jewels date from the right period of history—the Bronze Age, about 2200 B.C. But did Schliemann really find the large treasure at Troy? And if so, did it really have any connection with the Trojan War?

In May 1873, he found what he decided had been the treasure of Priam, the old Trojan king. Schliemann said he came upon it when the workmen had left the site—that he dug it out himself, at great danger from subsiding earth, with only his young Greek wife Sophie to help him. This cannot be true. Sophie was away in Athens at the time. Most likely he found the objects over a period of several days and kept them secret until he could get them out of Turkey. He did not want to share them with the Turkish government as he had promised to do.

The treasure was genuine enough: thousands of gold rings, along with gold bracelets, earrings, and diadems. One diadem was composed of 16,000 tiny pieces of gold. Excitedly Schliemann declared that these must have been the jewels of the fabled Helen. There is a photograph of Sophie wearing them.

But where are they now? Nobody knows. They were taken to Berlin. When Hitler started World War II they were moved, like many other

priceless objects, to some bomb-proof storage place. But in May 1945, when the Red Army battered its way into Berlin and Hitler committed suicide in his concrete bunker, the so-called jewels of Helen disappeared and have never yet been traced.

Where is it now? The treasure from Troy was on display in Berlin—but it disappeared in 1945. Will it ever be found again?

11

The famous Lion Gate, entrance to the royal palace at Mycenae, dates from about 1350 B.C. and is one of the oldest examples of prehistoric Greek sculpture. The square opening below is about twelve feet (three and a half meters) wide and high. Through this we can imagine King Agamemnon setting out for the siege of Troy, and, ten years later, returning victorious, dismounting from his chariot, and going up the steps that then led into the palace—there to be murdered by his unfaithful queen and her lover. The story is presented in the ancient play Agamemnon, *by Aeschylus.*

FACT BOX

Mycenae was the most important city in Greece between about 1500 and 1000 B.C.

The city was later itself destroyed, by armies from Argos in 468 B.C., but its massive ruins always remained in view.

Schliemann began excavating here in 1876.

He discovered splendid treasures, which can be seen in the National Museum at Athens.

Troy had been forgotten for ages and had to be found again. But people had always known the location of Mycenae, the city of the mighty King Agamemnon, who had sailed across the sea to attack the Trojans.

Schliemann had visited Mycenae two years before he began to dig at Troy. A rocky spur jutted out from the high mountains, dropping into rugged ravines and looking across the fertile plain to the sea. On it stood the tumbled ruins of the proud city, "golden Mycenae of the wide ways," deserted since 468 B.C., when it had been destroyed by invading armies.

A magical spot, Mycenae. But Schliemann was intent on finding Troy, and it was eight years later—1876—before he came back. He had fallen out with the Turkish government. For the moment they would not let him go on digging at Troy. So, with the permission of the Greek government, he turned to Mycenae instead.

12

The Treasure of Mycenae

Its massive Lion Gate—so called because of the two carved lions that still crowned it, their front paws resting on an altar with a sacred pillar set between them—still rose against the sky. There were walls too, called cyclopean walls. The blocks were so huge that surely only giants, like Cyclops in Homer's poem the *Odyssey*, could ever have laid one upon another.

Schliemann began with the Lion Gate and cleared it of debris. Just inside, he told his gang of laborers to dig a deep trench. September turned into October, and then the rains of November turned the site into a quagmire of mud. But Schliemann was undaunted. He was beginning to find things—upright slabs of stone carved with figures. When the mud was wiped away he could make them out clearly. He saw helmeted warriors in chariots, just like the heroes Homer described in the *Iliad*, fighting below the ramparts of Troy.

These two-inch (five centimeters) golden discs, exquisitely patterned with sea creatures and other designs, were probably fastened to women's dresses like huge sequins.

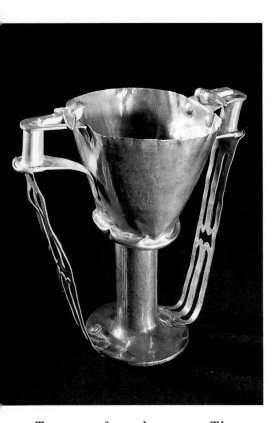

Treasures from the graves. The golden cup, or vase, is known as Nestor's Cup because it resembles the one described by Homer in the Iliad as used by the elderly king of that name. Many articles (like the oval seal) show hunting scenes. With so many rings and pins and buttons the ladies needed boxes in which to keep them.

The slabs were like gravestones. They had been arranged to form a continuous wall, as if to guard something. But what?

Schliemann soon found out. His men at last cut down through the soil to the unbroken bedrock beneath. But in places that rock *had* been broken—by the tools of other workmen thousands of years before. He could see the top of an oblong shaft going down into the depths. As his men went on digging, no fewer than five such shafts were revealed.

It had been golden Mycenae indeed. Here were gold and silver drinking cups and gold boxes. There were hundreds of little gold discs—spirals and rosettes, fishes and beasts—once stitched to cloth that had long since rotted away.

There were swords and daggers. The blades were of bronze, for gold would have been too soft to stand the stress of battle. The hilts were heavily gilded. And the bronze blades were inlaid with vivid scenes of combat and lion hunts, depicted in gold and silver and lapis lazuli. Schliemann saw the vanished world of Homer's poems come to life again before his eyes.

Two of the golden masks covering the faces of the dead men. These unknown princes lived before Agamemnon, with whom Schliemann mistakenly tried to connect them.

The shafts had been graves. The skeletons still lay there. Two of the dead had been ladies of high rank. They wore frontlets of gold on their foreheads, and one had a diadem. There were three men, too, their faces covered with golden masks fashioned like portraits. Under one mask the skull of the long-dead ruler was still in place.

Was it Agamemnon's? It is said that Schliemann persuaded himself that he had "looked upon the face of Agamemnon." He would have liked to believe it. But if he did so he was certainly wrong. More scientific methods have corrected him. We know now that the skeletons date from an earlier period than the Trojan War. But we still owe a great debt to Schliemann's patience and enthusiasm.

This treasure takes its name from the Oxus River (now called the Amu-Darya), which flows between Afghanistan and the Soviet Union.

It consists of gold articles and Greek coins, dating from the period 600–175 B.C. The older items may have been first collected by a Greek soldier in the army of Alexander the Great, who marched through this area about 334 B.C.

No one knows how it was found. Captain Francis Charles Burton saw it in 1880, before merchants went on to sell it at Rawalpindi, in what is now Pakistan.

Today the British Museum holds about 180 items.

The Oxus treasure included many representations of people and animals.

"Captain sahib!" The whisper was low but urgent. Captain Francis Burton was instantly alert.

You had to be—in these wild mountains. Even if deeply asleep you had to wake ready for anything, or you were not likely to live long.

Afghanistan has always been dangerous country, in 1880 it was particularly unstable. "What's up?" Burton demanded.

An exhausted man had just reached his camp. He was the servant of three merchants making the long journey down through the Khyber Pass to the Indian trading town of Rawalpindi. Like fools, they had not waited to travel in convoy with an armed escort, and so were captured by bandits. The servant had escaped and gone in search of help.

Burton had no troops with him. He was serving as a political officer, helping to govern this lawless region. But he knew he must do something. Taking only his two orderlies, he set off at once to track down the bandits.

It was a desperate mission. He knew what these mountain tribesmen were like— hawk-eyed fighters, crack shots with their long-barreled rifles, deadly at close quarters with their razor-keen scimitars and daggers.

That night, however, Burton was in luck. The robbers had not gone far from the road. They had taken the merchants and their laden mules to a nearby cave. They had started quarreling among themselves over dividing the loot.

When Burton reached the cave mouth, revolver at the ready, four of the thieves were sprawling wounded among the scattered contents of the merchants' baggage. This was no ordinary merchandise. Everywhere, even in that dim light, he caught the glint of gold.

Burton saw that he must play it carefully. With only his two orderlies he could not possibly arrest such a gang. So he struck a bargain. The merchants were set free and some of their goods handed back to them.

The Treasure of the Oxus

Burton knew that if he started back in the dark he might be ambushed, so he and his little party hid until dawn. Back at camp, he proclaimed that if the thieves did not return the other loot they would be hunted down. Soon three-quarters of the stolen goods were brought in.

It was a rich hoard, nearly all gold. There was a model of a four-horse chariot, magnificent golden armlets, a scabbard depicting a lion hunt, a silver statuette of a Persian king, and hundreds of glistening coins.

The merchants said it had all been dug up near the Oxus River. Burton bought an armlet. Then the men went on their way. They sold the treasure, bit by bit, in the bazaars of Rawalpindi. For several years separate items kept turning up. Sir Alexander Cunningham bought every item he could. Some perhaps were melted down or sold elsewhere.

It was quite literally only the first step.

Howard Carter found it when he was clearing the site of some ancient workmen's huts on the rocky hillside just below the tomb of Rameses VI.

For years he had worked in Egypt, starting as a boy of seventeen. He had excavated in the Valley of the Kings for a rich American, Theodore Davis. When Davis gave up hope of finding anything more, Carter sought help from the wealthy earl of Carnarvon. Although only an enthusiastic amateur, for sixteen years the earl took an active share in the quest, as well as financing it. But on this memorable day he was far away in England.

The laborers' shovels had revealed the top step of a staircase that clearly went down into the ground.

Such a staircase often led to the entrance of a tomb. All that day, and the next, the laborers worked hard—but very carefully—shifting the powdery earth from one step after another.

Carter knew what damage could be done if they went at the job too quickly. He was eager enough, but years of experience had taught him patience. He forced himself to go slowly, noting every detail. Like a detective at the scene of a murder, he had to make sure that no evidence was destroyed.

The staircase was becoming an underground passage, seven feet (two meters) wide, ten feet (three meters) high.

FACT BOX

After the age of the pyramids the rulers of Egypt—the Pharaohs—chose for themselves tombs in the Valley of the Kings, in the Western Desert near Luxor, 600 miles (1,000 kilometers) up the Nile River.

Many were buried there between about 1567 B.C. and 1085 B.C. By 1922, sixty-one such tombs had been found, including some empty unfinished ones and some made for important courtiers. All had been opened by robbers at one time or another.

On November 4, 1922, after years of patient searching, Howard Carter discovered one more.

At the twelfth step down, to his delight, something fresh came into view. It was a lintel —the top of a doorway.

The digging went on, more carefully than ever. The upper part of the doorway could be seen. And it was shut with an ancient seal portraying a jackal and nine captives.

That seal indicated two things. This was a royal tomb—and no one had passed through that doorway for over 3,000 years.

Carter grew more and more excited. Every previous tomb had been broken into and robbed, either in ancient times or recent centuries, and the priceless treasures buried within had been lost forever. Was he at last going to discover one with its original contents still intact?

He made a hole in the door just large enough to shine a flashlight inside. He could see only another passage, piled high with stones and rubble, just as the royal servants would have left it, to protect their dead master from disturbance.

Howard Carter standing inside the innermost chamber, his back to the golden shrine of the king. Later he examined the actual body and removed the consecration oils.

Carter would gladly have pressed on, working night and day to find out what lay beyond. But he thought of his friend Carnarvon, who had borne so much expense during all the years of digging. It was only fair that the earl should also share in the great moment.

He covered up the door and staircase again and sent off a cable to England.

In 1922 air travel had barely started. Carnarvon and his daughter Evelyn had to come out by train and ship. It was almost three weeks before they arrived.

Only then could the staircase be uncovered again, the door opened, and the inner passage cleared of the debris that was heaped up to its roof. After about thirty feet (ten meters) the archeologists came to an inner door.

Carter broke a hole through it and thrust a lighted candle inside, to test the purity of the air. For some moments he stood in a dazed silence.

"Can you see anything?" asked the earl.

"Yes," said Carter. "*Wonderful* things!"

FACT BOX

Tutankhamen was king of Egypt from about 1333 B.C. to 1323 B.C.

He was only about eighteen when he died.

His tomb is unusual and important because its contents had not been disturbed. It took Carter ten years to remove and catalog them.

The treasure is now mainly in the Cairo museum, but the mummified body still rests in its outer coffin in the tomb.

5 Behind the Sealed Door

This pectoral takes the form of a magnificent golden vulture.

There *were* wonderful things. The underground chamber was full of them.

Six or seven hundred items! Many bore the king's name, Tutankhamen, inscribed in hieroglyphics. Each item had to be listed.

There was his golden throne, sparkling with semiprecious stones of different colors, its arms winged snakes, its legs those of a lion. The back portrayed him with his girl-wife, Ankhesenamun, in a pleated robe. She was rubbing his shoulders with scented oil.

There were three gilded couches shaped like fantastic animals.

Two matching statues in black wood, with helmets, kilts and sandals of gold, stood guard with staff and mace outside another sealed door. What were they guarding behind it?

This first room was only a splendid antechamber. And another, opening off one side, was merely a storeroom for more treasures. It had been broken into, probably soon after the burial, but little had been disturbed. The ancient seal on the outer door showed that no one had ever entered the tomb again.

The door between the statues led to an inner chamber. The body should still be there.

The scene from the back of the Pharaoh's throne, showing Tutankhamen and his wife.

A jar for perfumed ointment, in the form of a lion.

The golden mask of Tutankhamen.

But the outer rooms had to be carefully cleared first. Wonderfully preserved in the dry atmosphere, the objects could now so easily crumble or catch fire. Even electric lamps had to be used with utmost caution.

One chest, brightly painted with battles and hunting scenes, held the king's robes, gleaming with thousands of sequins and golden rosettes. One robe was buckled with a superb scarab, or sacred beetle, in turquoise and gold. A high priest's robe, covered with gold and silver stars, had a gilded leopard's head as a buckle.

There were alabaster perfume jars, bronze and gold torch stands, caskets and chairs, even parts of chariots. A memento of the king's childhood was a little chair of ebony, ivory, and gold. Because he had died young his tomb contained nothing like the vanished riches buried with the mightier Egyptian rulers. Even so it took seven weeks to remove everything.

At last the inner door could be carefully broken down. Behind it glittered a massive golden shrine nine feet (nearly three meters) high. Carter and Carnarvon could just squeeze between it and the wall.

For the next eighty-four days, it was like unpacking a gigantic mystery parcel. The shrine's panels—oak sheeted in gold, weighing anything from 560 to 1,680 pounds (254 to 762 kilos) were removed one by one.

Inside was a second shrine. And a third. And a fourth. Then the outer coffin, yellow quartzite, ten feet (three meters) long, its rose-pink granite lid weighing over 2,200 pounds (1,000 kilos). A second coffin: the king's own likeness fashioned in gold. Two further coffins, the innermost of solid gold.

They could gaze at last upon the well-preserved mummy of Tutankhamen, who had been lord of all these treasures but had died—possibly poisoned—while still in his teens. That final mystery remains unsolved.

The great ziggurat *or sacred mountain of Ur was built by King Ur-Nammu (who lived at some time between 2112–2004 B.C.) around a much smaller, older temple.*

FACT BOX

Ur lies in modern Iraq, close to the Euphrates River, between Baghdad and the Persian Gulf.

It was an important city in the ancient Sumerian civilization. By 3000 B.C. it covered nearly 300 acres (120 hectares) and had some 24,000 inhabitants.

The site of Ur was first located in 1854, but proper excavations began only in 1922, and were carried on for twelve years by C. L. (later Sir Leonard) Woolley. His finds are divided among museums in London, Philadelphia, and Baghdad.

The Death Pit dates from about 2500 B.C.

Christians, Jews, and Muslims are all taught that Abraham was a man of God. The Muslims call him Ibrahim. Ur was the city in which he was born.

For ages Ur was a lost city. Then, in 1854, its site was discovered. The chief landmark was a manmade hill, which proved to be a ziggurat, or sacred mountain. The Sumerians had built it up in brick terraces 100 feet (thirty meters) high. A temple of their moon god, Nanna, had once stood on the top.

Just when Howard Carter was making his discoveries in Egypt, Leonard Woolley was beginning his great work at Ur, which lasted from 1922 to 1934.

He had worked in Egypt, and in other places, and he had the same careful, scientific attitude as Carter. His own career as an archeologist had been interrupted by World War I, when he had worked in British intelligence and had spent two years as a prisoner of the Turks.

He was a man of immense energy and enthusiasm. He was up at dawn, supervising the workmen in the cool part of the day—and sometimes there were 400 on the job. Then he might be busy until two or three o'clock in the morning, writing down every detail of what had been found.

There were also important visitors to show around the site. Because he talked so well, explaining the finds so brilliantly, bringing the long-dead city to life and helping his visitors to imagine it in the days of its glory, Woolley was described by some as a showman.

He needed to be. He had no one like the earl of Carnarvon to finance his project. He had to raise funds from museums and universities and generous backers to pay for his excavations.

He had uncovered the graves of many ordinary people, buried with their own humble possessions. But somewhere, he knew, must be the tombs of their wealthy rulers. And in 1927, on the very last day of the digging season, he found a splendid golden dagger that showed him he was on the right track.

Leonard Woolley (1880–1960), distinguished archeologist, famous for his discoveries at Ur.

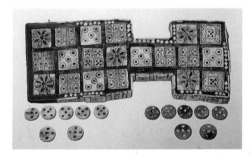

Beautifully inlaid gaming board, with its accompanying counters.

Golden dagger and sheath from the Royal Tombs, dated about 2500 B.C.

Gold headdress, with necklace of carnelian and lapis lazuli, worn by one of the dead women attendants.

Over the next few years he found no less than sixteen royal tombs close to the ziggurat.

One was that of Queen Pu-abi. It was strewn with gold and silver treasures. Before he reached it, he passed the skeletons of five guards with daggers—and then those of ten women in two neat rows, five and five, as though asleep.

They wore bead necklaces and golden headdresses with stones of carnelian and lapis lazuli. By pouring paraffin wax over these ornaments Woolley was able to preserve their original arrangement.

There were still more skeletons in this and other tombs, together with the bones of oxen and the four-wheel wagons they had pulled— and in one tomb a kind of decorated chariot. In a vault that he named the Great Death Pit, there were the remains of seventy-four courtiers and attendants.

They lay so neatly, with no signs of struggle. Their skulls had been smashed, but probably after they were dead. The key to the grim mystery was the little cup beside each body.

These people—chosen to serve their dead rulers in the next world—must have filed down into the tomb, lain down in their places, drunk from their drugged cups, and slipped into the sleep from which they never woke again.

Bull's head of gold, again with skillful use of lapis lazuli for the beard.

Mrs. Edith May Pretty often wondered about the eleven strange grassy mounds dotting the sandy heath above the Deben River on her Suffolk estate.

What lay under them? One old villager talked of treasure. Her own nephew, who had the gift of dowsing, or water divining, thought there might be buried gold.

In 1938 she sought the advice of the curator at the Ipswich Museum. Basil Brown came and dug into three of the mounds. He discovered human bones, traces of a boat, a blue glass bowl, and fragments of Anglo-Saxon pottery. So the mounds were not prehistoric but dated from about the year 600.

Next summer Mr. Brown came again. Mrs. Pretty pointed to the biggest mound. "What about this?" she said.

Mr. Brown's men started to dig a trench about six feet (two meters) wide across the mound. On the third day they found rusted nails in regular lines and the dark stains of vanished timbers tracing the shape of a good-sized vessel on the yellow sand. It finally proved to have been eighty-one feet (twenty-seven meters) long.

Very carefully they worked on. They removed the soil with a kitchen dustpan, so that no clue should be lost. After a month they reached a

Intricate patterns of little biting animals adorn the solid gold belt buckle, the finest piece of jewelry found. It is over five inches (thirteen centimeters) long and weighs fourteen and five-eighths ounces (414.62 grams).

The Treasure of the Wolf People

The archeologists found that the shape of the ship remained quite clearly marked in the sandy soil, though the timbers had long since rotted away.

This splendid little bronze stag surmounted a two-foot (sixty-one centimeters) stone bar, believed to have been a scepter.

burial chamber built amidships. Its roof of turf and timber had long ago fallen in.

It was time to call in the experts. Early in July, C. W. Phillips from Cambridge took charge with a team of specialists. It took three weeks to uncover the burial chamber and realize the richness of their find.

There were jewelry and silver plate, a gold-hilted sword, a helmet inlaid with silver and garnets—in all, 4,000 of those blood-red precious stones were found. Everything had to be listed and photographed. Mrs. Pretty kept

Animals, birds, and men, made from garnets, glass, and gold, decorate this purse lid. There were thirty-seven coins in the purse.

the chief treasures under her bed. A police guard was mounted to protect the site itself from looters.

There was no sign of a skeleton. Had the buried vessel been a king's tomb or his empty monument? It was not a Viking ship. Its contents indicated the early Anglo-Saxon period, when Suffolk was ruled by the Wuffingas, the Wolf People. It is now thought most likely that the king was the powerful Raedwald, who died about A.D. 625.

In Britain, when hidden gold or silver objects are found, an inquiry or inquest must be held by the coroner, as in the case of a mysterious death. Were they buried secretly? Did the owner intend to come back for them? If so, and if the owner cannot be traced, they count as treasure trove and belong to the present king or queen—though their cash value is usually paid to the finder.

On this occasion the inquest, held on August 14, 1939, decided that the hoard was not treasure trove, for it could not have been buried secretly and there was no sign that its owners had ever meant to come back for it. So it did not belong to King George VI but to Mrs. Pretty. A week later she announced that she was presenting it to the nation.

The following week, World War II started. So the treasure was at once buried again—in a disused part of the London Underground railway—to protect it from German bombs. Only after the war could it be displayed at last in the British Museum.

Helmet found in fragments and reconstructed. The crest is of iron, the eyebrows of bronze inlaid with garnets and silver wire, and the nose and mouth of gilded bronze.

FACT BOX

The treasure was found in January 1942 by Gordon Butcher and Sidney Ford.

The site: a plowed field (exact spot uncertain) at West Row, Mildenhall, Suffolk, twelve miles (nineteen kilometers) NW of Bury St. Edmunds.

There were thirty-four pieces of Roman silver tableware in fine condition, total weight about fifty-five pounds (twenty-five and a half kilos), dating from the fourth century A.D.

The treasure is now on view in the British Museum.

Early accounts of the Mildenhall treasure suggest a little mystery about its discovery—when, and by whom.

The treasure was turned up (as many similar finds have been) by someone plowing on a winter's day. It was wartime. People's minds were full of invasion scares and suspicions of Nazi spies. There was a warning poster, CARELESS TALK COSTS LIVES. People kept quiet about many things, and not every news story got into the papers.

Perhaps the finders did not at once realize that the items were valuable. Silver does not keep its brightness in the earth as gold does. This treasure, so brilliant today in the museum showcase, would have looked black and uninteresting when it first peeped through the furrowed soil. It had lain there for 1,500 years.

Still, the farm workers took the trouble to

The Treasure of Mildenhall

search for other pieces. In the end they found thirty-four—dishes, goblets, bowls, plates, and thin-handled spoons. But they did not report them at once to the police as they should have done. When at last they did so, after the war, and an inquest in 1946 declared the items treasure trove, they forfeited the full reward because of this long delay.

The treasure came into the possession of the British Museum. When the experts got to work on the silver and its full beauty was revealed, they saw that it was one of the finest such discoveries ever made in Britain.

It dated from the last period of the Roman occupation, when eastern areas like Suffolk were often raided by heathen Saxons from across the North Sea. That is probably why it was buried, and its owner did not live to come back for it.

Dish and spoons from the great silver treasure found at Mildenhall.

The showpiece is a great dish about two feet (sixty centimeters) in diameter and eighteen pounds (over eight kilos) in weight. In the center is the staring face of a sea god, with a spreading beard of seaweed, and dolphins darting out of his long wild hair. Whirling around him is a ring of figures from myth and legend, Bacchus and Hercules and Pan, nymphs and satyrs, dancing and playing musical instruments.

The plates and bowls are decorated with equal artistry. But in contrast with these pagan scenes, five of the eight spoons are obviously Christian in character.

Three bear the Greek capital letters *XP*. In the Greek alphabet *X* is sounded like our *Ch* in *Christ*, and the Greek *P* is our *R*. So the monogram really spells *CHR* and stands for *Christ*.

Christianity did not become the official state religion of Rome until the year 380. But many people had already adopted it before then. The experts date the items from the period roughly 360 to 370, when a home might well contain a mixture of pagan and Christian items.

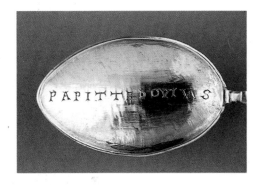

Another spoon bears the Latin words *PAPITTEDO VIVAS*, "May you live long, Papittedo!" It was probably a christening spoon such as babies are often given today. And another spoon is inscribed *PASCENTIA* and could have been for the baptism of a girl of that name.

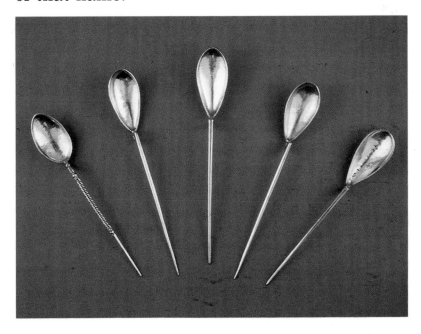

An adventurous American explorer, John Lloyd Stephens, was the first discoverer of the ancient city of Chichén Itzá and the wonderful Mayan civilization that had existed in Central America long before Columbus landed in the New World. The Aztecs of Mexico and the Incas of Peru were always remembered because they still had powerful empires that the Spaniards had to fight and overthrow. But the great days of the Maya were long past by 1492, and in time their ruined cities were forgotten and overgrown by the jungle.

Stephens proved that the Maya had not been savages but great builders and planners and skillful craftsmen. An English artist, Frederick Catherwood, went with him, sketching the spectacular ruins they came upon in the wilderness—for in those days the camera had just been invented.

Chichén Itzá had been one of the greatest cities. There had been a terraced pyramid surmounted by a temple to the god Kukulcán, the Plumed Serpent (who was the same as Quetzalcoatl, worshiped by the Mexican Aztecs). There had been a vast ball court, in which crowds had watched a game somewhat like basketball.

The ball was made of solid rubber (unknown to Europe at that time) and it had to be knocked through a stone ring high on the wall. It was very difficult, because players could not use their hands—only their forearms or knees, shoulders or hips. Gruesome sculptures show the losing side having their heads chopped off. One hopes that this was not the usual ending of a match! But the Toltecs, who took over Chichén Itzá, seem to have been even more cruel than the Maya.

Both used the Well of Sacrifice, which lay at the end of a causeway 900 feet (274 meters) long, stretching from the center of the city.

A frog-shaped gold pendant.

FACT BOX

Chichén Itzá lies on the Yucatan peninsula of Mexico.

The first city was built by the Maya about 800. A new city was built by their conquerors, the warlike Toltecs, in 987. They ruled until about 1180.

The ruins were described by John L. Stephens and Frederick Catherwood in 1843, and were first excavated in 1875.

The Well of Sacrifice was first investigated in 1904, and more scientifically in 1962.

The clifflike side of the enormous sacred well was only one of the many obstacles Edward Herbert Thompson faced.

Thompson in 1907, standing by the winding gear of the dredge he used to scoop treasure from the well.

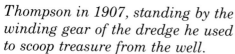

It is actually a large pool of greenish-black water, 200 feet (sixty meters) across. It has sheer sides of rock, falling dramatically to the pool deep below.

In Yucatan there are very few streams or rivers, because the rain goes straight through the limestone rock and carves out underground caverns and watercourses. Where the roof of such a cavern has collapsed, a well, or *cenote*, is revealed with water at the bottom—which is the main source of supply to the local inhabitants.

During a drought the level might fall dangerously low. People would make prayers and sacrifices to the rain god. The great *cenote* at Chichén Itzá drew pilgrims from far and wide.

It was an obvious place to search for treasure. In 1904 an American, Edward Herbert Thompson, decided to use deep-sea diving techniques. He equipped himself with air compressors and dredging gear, and even brought over two sponge fishermen from Greece to help him.

For days he found nothing. Then, when he was on the point of giving up, his search was rewarded. Little jade figures, rings and pendants of the same material, tiny bells of copper, stone knives, and ornamental discs of gold were found. Also found were the skeletons of the hapless people who had been sacrificed, thrown from the cliff walls that enclosed the dark pool. So far forty-two skeletons have been recovered, half of them children's, many very young.

In 1962 a more scientific search was sponsored by the National Geographic Society. Over 4,000 fresh objects were found, many of jade. The gold discs were very thin, the total weight in gold totaling only fifteen pounds (seven kilos), but they were embossed with scenes that told much about Mayan and Toltec customs.

Over 200 bells were found in the well. Most were made of copper, but some, like this monkey holding his tail, were made of gold.

Several jade tablets carved with human figures were discovered. Jade was highly prized by the Maya.

Tiny figures of fantastic animals can be found among the craggy peaks of the mountain that tops this incense burner. Found in Liu Sheng's tomb, the incense burner is made of bronze.

FACT BOX

The tombs were discovered in 1968 at Mancheng, ninety miles (150 kilometers) SW of Peking (now Beijing). They belong to the period of the Han emperors, 206 B.C. to A.D. 220.

They were built for Prince Liu Sheng before he died, 113 B.C., and for his wife Tou Wan.

2,800 items, including gold and silver, were found; most important were the burial suits of jade. They are now in the Peking Palace Museum.

Soldiers, idly strolling on the little hill above the town, were the first to notice the stone chippings on its bare slope. They were not recently made. They seemed to suggest some work done long ago. But why up here, at this particular spot? Experts thought that an ancient tomb might lie beneath. Soldiers and local people were set to dig.

There proved to be two tombs, the second not far from the first. One had been that of Prince Liu Sheng, brother of the mighty emperor Wu-ti. The prince was lazy and pleasure-loving. "A true king," he said, "should pass his days delighting himself with beautiful sights and sounds."

The other tomb was for the prince's wife and cousin, Princess Tou Wan.

The prince had had them made during his lifetime—the best way to make sure that the tremendous task was done. Even with several hundred laborers, the hewing of the rock must have meant at least a year's work.

Later, when the royal couple died and were buried, the mouth of each tomb was blocked with heavy stones. Then iron was melted on the site and poured over the entrances, so that when the metal cooled the tombs were sealed with a barrier of solid iron.

The gentle slope of the hill above the prince's tomb made it possible to get into it by digging a shaft down from above. The archeologists were lowered into the dark vault beneath. Shining their flashlights, they found that the tomb consisted of a main chamber, over twenty feet (seven meters) high, three smaller side chambers, and a long passage leading to the blocked entrance in the hillside.

One of these smaller chambers contained the remains of several chariots and the skeletons of a dozen horses. In another were hundreds of jars that had once held food and wine.

More than one and a half pounds (700 grams) of gold wire were used to stitch together Princess Tou's jade suit.
Was this the sacred lake of el dorado, "the golden man"? We cannot be sure, but Guatavita, in Colombia, is a favorite choice.

There were many other, more splendid, objects. A bronze sword, an iron dagger with gold-bound hilt, a bronze lamp in the shape of a ram, a vase inlaid with gold and silver, another vase adorned with dragons sailing through the clouds—even gold and silver needles for the ancient Chinese medical treatment of acupuncture.

The most interesting find looked, at first sight, like a heap of little jade tablets jumbled on the floor. When picked up, they were found to be joined together with gold wire, threaded through tiny holes drilled in the hard stone.

The experts became excited. The ancient Chinese had believed that jade could prevent the decay of the dead body. It was recorded that men had been buried in whole suits of the material, linked like chain mail, but none had ever been found. Could this clinking bundle of thin stone scales be such a garment?

Meanwhile, there was the second tomb. It was difficult to dig into this one from above. How could that iron wall blocking the entrance be dealt with? The archeologists allowed the army to use a method that would have horrified the archeologists of the West. Dynamite! The iron barrier was shattered. The experts went in to discover an even larger tomb in the heart of the hill.

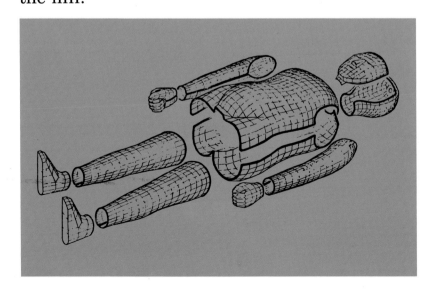

The suit was made in twelve pieces, as this diagram shows.

These leopards were used as weights.

Its contents were in some ways different, but just as interesting. There were beautiful bronze lamps, one held by the statue of a palace maidservant. There was a gold-inlaid incense burner with a lid portraying hunters in pursuit of game. There were tiny leopards of bronze inlaid with silver and garnets. There was the actual pillow—gilded bronze and jade, its end shaped like deer heads—on which the head of the dead princess had rested.

Next to it was her empty, tumbled suit of jade.

For of course the jade had not been able to prevent the decay of the bodies. Prince and princess had long ago turned to dust. But those funeral suits remained, the gold wire still holding the tiny tablets of stone together, 2,690 for the prince's, 2,156 for Tou Wan's. Each suit was in twelve parts, including shoes and gloves.

Dummy figures were carefully made to the right measurements. Then the original sections of the garments were fitted around them, piece by piece.

And it was as though Liu Sheng and his princess had come back.

A gold model of a raft carrying participants in the El Dorado ceremony. The model itself was used as an offering.

The world is full of treasure that awaits finding.

In England, King John's crown and jewels may still lie somewhere in the once marshy farmlands on the coast of the Wash, where his baggage convoy was overwhelmed by a sudden tidal flood in 1216.

In southern Italy lies the fabulous hoard of Alaric, king of the Goths, who looted Rome in 410 and then died of fever. His chieftains dammed the course of the Busento River, buried him with his plunder, and released the water again to flow over his grave. The digging party were slaughtered so that the spot would remain secret.

Antony and Cleopatra are believed to lie in a very different kind of burial place—their tomb is probably deep beneath the sprawling city of Alexandria and may one day come to light when foundations are dug for some vast modern office building or hotel, just as a Roman temple to the god Mithras was discovered in the heart of London.

What happened to the fabulous Peacock Throne of the Mogul emperors of India—a throne adorned with 108 large rubies, 116 emeralds, countless diamonds, and row upon row of splendid pearls? It was looted from Delhi in 1739 by the Persian conqueror Nadir Shah, and was never seen again, though it was said to be kept safe in the royal treasure house at Tehran.

And there is the Eldorado legend, of the lake in South America, where *el dorado*, "the golden man," was an Indian king coated from head to foot in gold dust, in whose honor rich offerings of the metal were thrown into the water. Some think that this is Lake Guatavita in Colombia. Attempts have been made to drain it, and some gold has been found, but the Colombian government has now proclaimed it a protected area of natural and cultural interest, and further searches are forbidden.

Islands are favorite hiding places in stories. One real island is Cocos in the Pacific, 400 miles (over 600 kilometers) from the South American coast. In 1820 there was a revolution in Peru, and a group of rich people in Lima loaded their wealth into a ship, the *Mary Deare*, hoping to escape to Spain. The Scottish captain, William Thompson, is said to have tricked them and buried the treasure on this mountainous little island, but in spite of searches it has never yet been found.

The collapse of Nazi Germany in World War II gave rise to several treasure stories. The German general in North Africa, Field Marshal Rommel, had a war chest of gold and diamonds for use in regions where paper money would not be accepted. When driven out of Africa by the British and Americans in 1943, he put this treasure in a submarine and sent it to Corsica, a French island still held by the Germans. It was landed secretly and buried in the maquis, the scrubby undergrowth that covers the Corsican hills. On its voyage back, the U-boat was sunk with all hands by the American navy. Thus, this secret, too, was lost—but many a Corsican believes that the gold and diamonds are still there and that some lucky person will find them.

Luck like that can happen to anyone—and close to home just as possibly as in far-off places. So it is always worth keeping one's eyes open. One never knows.

Glossary

alabaster a smooth marble-like stone
Anglo Saxons Germanic tribes that invaded Britain after the Romans
archeology study of ancient objects
Bacchus Roman god of wine
carnelian a semiprecious stone
diadem a jeweled headband
dowsing water-divining method that may also detect metals
effigy dummy figure of a human being in metal, stone or wood
frontlet a decorative band worn on the forehead
garnet a deep red semiprecious stone
Hercules ancient Greek hero
hieroglyphics Egyptian picture script
Homer early Greek poet, supposed to have composed (not written) the *Iliad* and the *Odyssey*
Iliad long poem about siege of Troy
jade a hard blue, green, or white stone
lapis lazuli a blue stone
lintel the top of a doorway
mummy a dead body preserved and bandaged according to ancient Egyptian practice, to prevent its decay
nymph in Greek myth a spirit, like a beautiful girl, inhabiting the mountains, woods, rivers, or the sea
Odyssey long poem about the return of the Greeks from Troy
Pan Greek and Roman god of the woodland
pectoral an ornament worn on the chest
pharaoh a king of Egypt
plaque an ornamental tablet of metal or stone or porcelain
quartzite a hard kind of rock
satyr in Greek myth a woodland creature, part man and part horse or goat
scarab Egyptian gem cut in form of sacred beetle
sequin small ornament, usually round, sewn onto cloth
stratum layer of soil or rock
turquoise blue or green semiprecious stone
Viking sea raider from Scandinavia
ziggurat a Sumerian pyramid rising in steps

Index